U.S. COAST GUARD

A B SEAS

Written by

John Fitzgerald & Audrey Gaynier

Illustrated by

Audrey Gaynier

The views expressed herein are those of the authors and are not to be considered as official or reflecting the views of the U.S. Coast Guard Commandant or the U.S. Coast Guard.

All characters appearing in this work are fictitious. Any resemblance to real persons, living or dead, is purely coincidental.

All rights reserved.

No part of this book may be reproduced in any manner without the express written consent of the publisher, except in the case of brief excerpts in critical reviews and articles.

Text copyright @ 2024 John Fitzgerald
Illustrations copyright @ 2024 Audrey Gaynier

ISBN: 979-8-9892284-1-6

The three Coast Guard pioneers represented on the front cover are:

Alex Haley

Served in the Coast Guard for 20 years (1939-1959) and was the Coast Guard's first Chief Journalist. An accomplished writer, he wrote the award winning novel, Roots.

Ida Lewis

A famous lighthouse keeper at Lime Rock Light in Rhode Island, she conducted her first rescue at the age of 12 in 1854 and served as a lighthouse keeper for over 50 years.

Elmer Stone

In 1917, he completed naval flight training and became Coast Guard aviator number one, the Coast Guard's first pilot.

A is for Aircraft

The Coast Guard often uses airplanes and helicopters to respond to emergencies. When aircraft arrive on scene, they can hoist people to safety or drop rescue equipment.

B is for Buoy

The Coast Guard places buoys in the water so ships can safely travel in and out of port. Most buoys are red or green but can be other colors too. Some buoys have lights or bells so they can be found at night and in the fog.

Coast Guard ships that work with buoys are called buoy tenders. Buoy tenders are painted black so when they drag buoys and chains on board they do not look dirty. Other Coast Guard ships are usually painted red or white.

C is for Cutter

Coast Guard ships are called cutters. Hundreds of years ago, cutters were powered by the wind. Today, they have powerful engines that allow them to quickly respond to an emergency.

D is for Diver

Coast Guard divers go underwater with air tanks to inspect and repair cutters in remote areas. Divers often see fish, marine mammals and other sea life. Sometimes curious animals watch the divers from above.

E is for Eagle

The Coast Guard sailing ship Eagle is used to teach Coast Guard women and men about the sea. It is mainly powered by twenty three sails.

The crew sets all of the sails on Eagle by hand. Sometimes sailors have to climb the rigging or "go aloft" to set the sails. The two biggest masts on Eagle are over 145 feet tall.

H is for Helicopter

Coast Guard helicopters perform search and rescue. They usually take off with a rescue swimmer who can help people on both land and at sea.

Rescue swimmers are lowered onto a vessel or into the water using the helicopter's hoist. Other times, the rescue swimmer will jump out of the open helicopter door and splash into the water.

I is for Iceberg

The Coast Guard patrols the north Atlantic Ocean to warn ships of icebergs in their path. Sometimes, Coast Guard aircraft drop different colored paint on the icebergs to identify them.

Every year, on the anniversary of the Titanic's collision with an iceberg, the Coast Guard lays a remembrance wreath at the site of the cruise liner's sinking.

L is for Lighthouse

Lighthouses help guide ships and keep them in safe water. Many lighthouses also sound a horn to warn sailors in the fog or bad weather. The Coast Guard makes sure the lights and sound devices in lighthouses work properly.

M is for Motor Lifeboat

Along the coast where there are rough seas, the Coast Guard has motor lifeboats ready to respond. These boats are specifically built to keep the crew safe. If they flip over, they will turn right-side up in under a minute.

N is for North Star

Out at sea, Coast Guard ships use the North Star to navigate. It is easily seen in the constellation called the Little Dipper. The North Star always indicates which direction is north.

Sailors also use a special tool called a sextant to help them navigate. With a sextant, you can use the stars, planets, sun, and moon to locate your position.

O is for Orange

Since the sky and water are blue, bright orange can be easily seen by rescuers. Therefore, Coast Guard helicopters and life saving equipment are bright orange.

Coast Guard cutters that sail in frigid waters also carry exposure suits which protect the crew from the cold. Coast Guard crews jokingly call them "gumby suits."

P is for Port (and Starboard)

The left side of a ship or boat is called the "port" side and at night it shows a red light. The right hand side is called the "starboard" side and it displays a green light at night.

Q is for Queen of the Fleet

U.S. COAST GUARD CUTTER
SMILAX
WAGL 315
COSMOS CLASS INLAND CONSTRUCTION TENDER
BUILT BY DUBUQUE BOAT & BOILER WORKS
DUBUQUE, IOWA
KEEL LAID   NOV 26, 1943
LAUNCHED   AUG 18, 1944
COMMISSIONED   NOV 1, 1944

The Coast Guard's oldest commissioned cutter is called the "Queen of the Fleet." It is the only cutter whose hull numbers are painted gold.

R is for Rescue

Every year, the Coast Guard rescues hundreds of people. They use aircraft, cutters, and small boats to quickly arrive on scene and provide assistance.

One famous rescue occurred in 2008 in the Bering Sea. Coast Guard Cutter Munro and two helicopters rescued 20 people from the fishing vessel Alaska Ranger.

S is for Station

Coast Guard Stations are located along the Atlantic, Pacific and Gulf coasts, on the Great Lakes, and in some U.S territories. They have personnel standing by to respond to any sign of distress, such as a flare or mayday call.

The earliest Coast Guard station crews would row their boats out to sea to rescue sailors whose ships had run aground or sank offshore.

V is for Voyage

When a Coast Guard cutter takes a trip, it is called a voyage. Some cutters have taken voyages around the world and others have gone to the North and South Poles.

Every year before Christmas, the Coast Guard Cutter Mackinaw makes a special voyage. Mackinaw sails from her home port near the Straits of Mackinaw and travels down Lake Michigan to deliver over 1,000 Christmas trees to families in Chicago.

W is for Weather

Coast Guard personnel always keep track of the weather. Hurricanes, storms, rain, snow and high winds can put people on or near the water in danger.

During the winter, Coast Guard icebreakers also monitor conditions on major waterways. When necessary, they break the ice and keep ports open so ships can safely transport their cargo.

X is for X Marks The Spot

Nautical maps are called charts. The crew on watch will mark the ship's position on a chart with an "X." Hundreds of years ago, pirates buried their treasure and used an "X" to mark the spot on a map.

Y is for Yard

The Coast Guard Yard in Baltimore, Maryland is where ships go for inspections and repairs. At the yard, cutters are taken out of the water using huge wooden blocks and water pumps.

Z is for Zebra

While a zebra is an animal, it is also the term used when cutters close every door and window to "batten down the hatches." Cutters set condition "zebra" when sailing in dangerous waters or during an on-board emergency.

U.S. Coast Guard: Did You Know?

A is for Aircraft: The Coast Guard has approximately 200 fixed wing and rotary aircraft in its inventory.

B is for Buoy: In one year, the Coast Guard services nearly 50,000 aids to navigation. The seasonal Francis Scott Key buoy near Baltimore is painted like the American Flag.

C is for Cutter: A cutter is a vessel greater than 65 feet in length. The Coast Guard has a fleet of over 250 cutters.

D is for Diver: Coast Guard polar icebreakers have Navy certified divers who dive under the ice to assist scientists with polar experiments.

E is for Eagle: The Barque Eagle, built in Germany in 1936, was originally used to train German sailors. It was obtained by the U.S. Coast Guard after World War II.

F is for Flags: The Coast Guard has two flags. The one for parades is primarily blue with a white background. The one for units is white with red vertical stripes.

G is for Galley: Other nautical terms include: ladders which are stairs; a head is a bathroom; and a porthole is a window.

H is for Helicopter: nearly 75% of the Coast Guard's aircraft are helicopters.

I is for Iceberg: A C-130 ice patrol flight is usually between five to seven hours long and covers roughly 30,000 square miles.

J is for Jayhawk: Jayhawk helicopters have a range of approximately 700 nautical miles and a maximum speed of 170 knots.

K is for Knot: Common knots include the bowline, square knot and clove hitch. A knot is also the term used when measuring nautical miles traveled per hour.

L is for Lighthouse: While Alcatraz Island is famous for its prison, it also has a lighthouse that guides ships in San Francisco Bay.

M is for Motor Lifeboat: Motor Lifeboats are 47-feet in length. Coxswains who drive these boats learn to operate them in heavy seas at the National Motor Lifeboat School in Cape Disappointment, Washington.

N is for North Star: Mariners can fix their position using the sun, stars and planets in a few minutes. Today, most ships use satellites to determine their position within a few seconds.

O is for Orange: The Coast Guard's distinctive racing stripe on its ships, aircraft and boats was first authorized in 1967.

P is for Port (and Starboard): In addition to port and starboard, the front part of a ship is called the bow and the back part is called the stern. The bottom is called the keel.

Q is for Queen of the Fleet: In 2024, the Queen of the Fleet was the Coast Guard Cutter Smilax which was commissioned in 1944.

R is for Rescue: Cutter Munro is named after Signalman First Class Douglas Munro who was awarded the Medal of Honor for his heroic actions at Guadalcanal during World War II.

S is for Station: The Coast Guard has approximately 180 small boat stations throughout the United States and its territories.

T is for Towing: Some Coast Guard cutters carry a tow line which is over a football field in length.

U is for Uniform: The Coast Guard and Navy use the same rank structure for both officers and enlisted personnel.

V is for Voyage: The first Coast Guard vessel to circumnavigate the globe was Coast Guard Cutter Eastwind in 1962.

W is for Weather: The Coast Guard assists the National Oceanic and Atmospheric Administration (NOAA) by placing weather buoys out at sea. These buoys provide data to meteorologists so they can provide more accurate forecasts.

X is for X Marks the Spot: Charts detail prominent points of land, water depth and the type of sea bottom which is important for anchoring and navigation. Many of today's charts are no longer paper but electronic.

Y is for Yard: The Coast Guard Yard was officially established in 1905.

Z is for Zebra: There are three readiness conditions that Coast Guard cutters can set: X-Ray, Yoke and Zebra. Zebra is the most secure.

About the Author

Capt. John Fitzgerald, USCG (ret.) graduated from the U.S. Coast Guard Academy in 1987 and served on active duty for 25 years. John also received his master's degree in Mass Communication from Boston University in 1996.

A permanent cutterman, he served on four ships: MIDGETT, HAMILTON, LEGARE and commanded the 210-foot cutter CONFIDENCE.

Other tours of duty included Commanding Officer of LORAN Station Kure Island, Hawaii; Press Secretary to the Commandant of the Coast Guard; Atlantic Area / Fifth District Public Affairs Officer and the Commandant of Cadets at the U.S. Coast Guard Academy.

About the Illustrator

Audrey Gaynier is a 2017 graduate of the U.S. Coast Guard Academy. Following graduation, she served on board cutter DECISIVE as the Damage Control Assistant. She was then assigned to the Project Residence Office Gulf Coast, in support of the National Security Cutter Construction program. She now lives in Mobile, AL where she works on the USCG Offshore Patrol Cutter construction program.

A talented artist, Audrey has combined her love of the Coast Guard with her passion for painting, thus creating her chart art business; Chart Art By Aud (Instagram: @chartart_byaud).

Acknowledgements

The authors would like to thank our friends and family for their support in writing this book. Their input, feedback and critiques were invaluable.

In particular we would like to recognize Cindy and Matthew.

Also providing technical assistance were:

Bill M	Kiana K
Pat & Jo O	Helen & Brian G
Glenn & Angie	Terry N & Miranda F
Graham S	Kyndall & Andrew S
Tina D & Allie D	Kathy B
Christopher P	Amanda R
Patrick & Matt O	Meghan & Mike P
Nancy & Joe M	Jenn C
JT	Emily G

The authors would also like to acknowledge the assistance provided by the U.S. Coast Guard in writing this book. Specifically, the personnel at the Coast Guard Motion Picture Office were invaluable in making the process easy and fun.

We hope you enjoyed our book. Please feel free to email us your comments at CGABSEAS@gmail.com.

This book is dedicated to all Coast Guard personnel, past and present, who have embodied the Service's core values of honor, respect and devotion to duty.

www.ingramcontent.com/pod-product-compliance
Lightning Source LLC
Chambersburg PA
CBHW061403010526
44119CB00010B/241